DOLPHINS

BOTTLENOSE DOLPHINS

JOHN F. PREVOST

ABDO & Daughters

Published by Abdo & Daughters, 4940 Viking Drive, Suite 622, Edina, Minnesota 55435.

Library bound edition distributed by Rockbottom Books, Pentagon Tower, P.O. Box 36036, Minneapolis, Minnesota 55435.

Printed in the United States.

Cover Photo credit: Peter Arnold, Inc.

Interior Photo credits: Peter Arnold, Inc.

Edited by Bob Italia

Library of Congress Cataloging-in-Publication Data

Prevost, John F.
    Bottlenose dolphins / by John F. Prevost.
        p.   cm. — (Dolphins)
Includes bibliographical references (p. 23) and index.
    ISBN 1-56239-493-2
1. Atlantic bottlenosed dolphin—Juvenile literature.
2. Bottlenosed dolphins—Juvenile literature.   [1. Bottlenosed dolphins. 2. Dolphins.]
I. Title. II . Series: Prevost, John F. Dolphins.
QL737.C432P74   1995
599.5'3—dc20   95-3316
                                                           CIP
                                                           AC

ABOUT THE AUTHOR

John Prevost is a marine biologist and diver who has been active in conservation and education issues for the past 18 years. Currently he is living inland and remains actively involved in freshwater and marine husbandry, conservation and education projects.

Contents

BOTTLENOSE DOLPHINS AND FAMILY

Bottlenose dolphins are small-toothed whales often seen in public **aquariums**. They are made for high-speed swimming. They use **echolocation** to find objects underwater.

Dolphins are **mammals**. They have some hair when born, are **warm blooded**, and **nurse** their young with milk. And like humans, they breathe air.

The name "bottlenose" describes the **snout** of these dolphins. Other dolphin family members are the 6-foot-long (2-meter-long) tucuxi dolphin, the 31-foot-long (9.5-meter-long) killer whale, and the 10-foot-long (3-meter-long) white-sided dolphin.

The name "bottlenose" describes the snout of these dolphins.

SIZE, SHAPE AND COLOR

Bottlenose dolphins may reach 13 feet (4 meters) long. The males are slightly larger than the females. Bottlenose are chunkier than other dolphins.

Bottlenose dolphins have many colors and markings. Most have dark gray backs. Some are bluish or even brown. The sides are lighter and the belly may be white or pink. Spots and faint stripes are found on some bottlenose dolphins. Other markings may include scrapes or **rake marks** from **social** action.

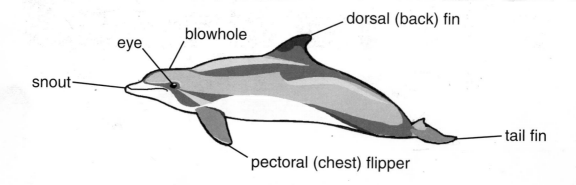

dorsal (back) fin

blowhole

eye

snout

tail fin

pectoral (chest) flipper

This bottlenose dolphin has a pink-colored belly.

WHERE THEY LIVE

Bottlenose dolphins are found in oceans all over the world except for the **polar** seas. There are two groups that have adjusted to their surroundings. One group is found along **coastlines**. These bottlenose dolphins stay in the same area year after year. But they may also travel into freshwater to follow **prey**.

The coastal bottlenose will form **pods** of about 12. Other bottlenose dolphin groups are found offshore. These animals will **migrate** to follow food. They often swim with other sea **mammals**.

Certain bottlenose dolphins are found along the coastline. Some dolphins stay in the same area year after year.

Open-water bottlenose will form larger **pods** with over 100 members. There are at least 3 **sub-species** of bottlenose dolphins. These groups are divided by **continents**.

SENSES

Bottlenose dolphins and people have 4 of the same senses. Hearing is their most important sense. Toothed whales use **echolocation**. By making a range of clicks and whistles, a bottlenose dolphin can "see" underwater by listening to the returning echoes.

HOW ECHOLOCATION WORKS

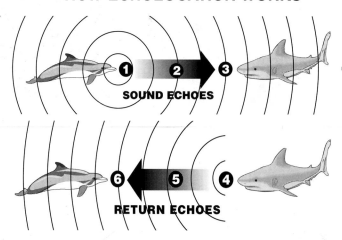

The dolphin sends out sound echoes (1). These echoes travel in all directions through the water (2). The sound echoes reach an object in the dolphin's path (3), then bounce off it (4). The return echoes travel through the water (5) and reach the dolphin (6). These echoes let the dolphin know where the object is, how large it is, and how fast it is moving.

Bottlenose dolphins can see well in and out of water.

Eyesight is also an important sense. Tests at public **aquariums** show that bottlenose dolphins can see well in and out of water. Touch is just as important to these **social** animals. Touching allows them to show feelings. Unlike humans, bottlenose dolphins do not have a sense of smell. But they do have the sense of taste.

DEFENSE

Bottlenose dolphins have few enemies: large sharks, killer whales, other **species** of toothed whales, and man. Swimming away from danger is their best defense. Some dolphins can travel up to 25 miles (40 kilometers) per hour for short bursts. They also can dive to 980 feet (300 meters).

The **pod** is also helpful. Within the group, more members can watch for **predators**. Young dolphins or **calves** are the most likely **prey**. But the mother and related females within the pod will care for and protect a calf.

The great white shark preys on dolphins.

FOOD

Bottlenose dolphins have 18 to 26 pairs of peg-shaped teeth on each jaw. These teeth are sharp and strong.

Bottlenose dolphins will often find their food with **echolocation**. To catch their food, bottlenose dolphins work together and **herd** their **prey**. If they are a **coastal** dolphin, fish may be chased into shallow water or even onto the beach! Offshore dolphins will herd fish or **squid** toward the water surface where the prey cluster and are easily captured.

To organize these activities, the dolphins **communicate** with each other with loud clicks and whistles that can be heard for long distances underwater.

Bottlenose dolphins work together to catch their food. Notice the peg-like teeth on these dolphins. Bottlenose dolphins have 18 to 26 pairs of teeth on each jaw.

BABIES

A baby bottlenose dolphin is called a **calf**. Bottlenose dolphins are **social** animals. This helps them safely raise dolphin calves. Other females in the **pod** will assist the mother by watching or "baby-sitting" while she is feeding. Often these females are related to the mother either as sisters or offspring. Adult males are rarely involved with the bottlenose calves.

Like other **mammals,** the mother gives milk to the calf which may **nurse** for as long as 18 months. The calf may eat fish and **squid** as early as 6 months.

A bottlenose dolphin and its calf swimming side-by-side.

BOTTLENOSE DOLPHIN FACTS

Scientific Name: *Tursiops truncatus*

Atlantic sub-species: *T. t. truncatus*

North Pacific sub-species: *T. t. gilli*

Indo-Pacific and Red Sea sub-species: *T. t. aduncus*

Average Size: 7.5 to 13 feet (2.3 to 4 meters)
Males are often larger than females, and the **sub-species**
are different in size.

Where They're Found: In oceans all over the world
except the **polar** seas. May travel briefly into freshwater.

NURSE - To feed a child or young animal from its mother's breasts.

POD - A herd or school of dolphins.

POLAR - Either the Arctic (north pole) or Antarctic (south pole) regions.

PREDATOR (PRED-uh-tor) - An animal that hunts and eats other animals.

PREY - Animals that are eaten by other animals.

RAKE MARKS - Scratches made by a dolphin's teeth on other dolphins.

SNOUT - The part of an animal's head that projects forward and includes the nose, mouth, and jaws.

SOCIAL - To live in organized groups.

SPECIES (SPEE-seas) - A plant or animal belonging to a particular classification.

SQUID - A group of sea animals related to the octopus that are streamlined in shape and have at least 10 arms.

SUB-SPECIES - A grouping of animals within a species.

WARM-BLOODED - An animal whose body temperature remains the same and warmer than the outside air or water temperature.

Index

BIBLIOGRAPHY

Cousteau, Jacques-Yves. *The Whale, Mighty Monarch of the Sea.* N.Y.: Doubleday, 1972.

Dozier, Thomas A. *Whales and Other Sea Mammals.* Time-Life Films, 1977.

Leatherwood, Stephen. *The Sierra Club Handbook of Whales and Dolphins.* San Francisco, California: Sierra Club Books, 1983.

Minasian, Stanley M. *The World's Whales.* Washington, D.C.: Smithsonian Books, 1984.

Ridgway, Sam H., ed. *Mammals of the Sea.* Springfield, Illinois: Charles C. Thomas Publisher, 1972.